Workbook

READY TO GO 1

Language • Lifeskills • Civics

Joan Saslow
Tim Collins

Workbook by
Barbara R. Denman

Longman

Ready to Go: Language, Lifeskills, Civics 1
Workbook

Pearson Education, 10 Bank Street, White Plains, NY 10606

Vice president, instructional design: Allen Ascher
Senior acquisitions editor: Marian Wassner
Senior development editor: Jessica Miller-Smith
Development editor: Julie Rouse
Vice president, director of design and production: Rhea Banker
Executive managing editor: Linda Moser
Production editor: Michael Mone
Ready to Go production editor: Marc Oliver
Production supervisor: Liza Pleva
Ready to Go production manager: Ray Keating
Director of manufacturing: Patrice Fraccio
Senior manufacturing buyer: Dave Dickey
Cover design: Ann France
Text design: Ann France
Text composition: Word and Image Design Studio Inc
Ready to Go text composition: Lehigh Press
Illustrations: Crowleart Group, p. 34; Brian Hughes, pp. 9, 17, 24, 26, 29, 42, 46, 48, 65,
    66, 72, 87; Dave McKay, pp.10 (top), 13, 15, 40; Suzanne Mogensen, pp. 3, 5, 10 (bottom),
    14, 37, 49, 50, 59; Allan Moon, pp. 21, 23, 33; Dusan Petricic, pp. 20, 28, 45; NSV
    Productions, pp. 1 (bottom), 36; Meryl Treatner, pp. 1 (top), 41, 62; Anna Veltfort, p. 24
Photography: Gilbert Duclos, pp. 7, 12

ISBN: 0-13-183456-8

Printed in the United States of America
1 2 3 4 5 6 7 8 9 10–BAH–05 04 03 02 01 00

Contents

UNIT 1
Your life

➤ Vocabulary

1 **Look at the picture. Write the letter on the line.**

1. __*b*__ a cook

2. _____ a bus driver

3. _____ a homemaker

4. _____ an engineer

5. _____ a housekeeper

6. _____ an electrician

7. _____ a cashier

8. _____ a mechanic

2 **Look at the pictures. Circle the letter.**

1. **a.** a student
   b. a mechanic
   c. a cashier

2. **a.** a plumber
   b. a homemaker
   c. an electrician

3. **a.** a housekeeper
   b. a mechanic
   c. a cook

4. **a.** an engineer
   b. a mechanic
   c. a plumber

3 Read. Choose your response. Circle the letter.

1. "Hi. I'm Ella. Are you Nancy?"

   a. N-A-N-C-Y

   (b.) Yes, I am. I'm Nancy Lewis.

2. "Where are you from, Alberto?"

   a. What about you?

   b. I'm from San Antonio.

3. "What do you do?"

   a. I'm a homemaker.

   b. No, I'm not.

4. "Nice to meet you, Ji-Soo."

   a. Yes, I am.

   b. Good to meet you, too.

4 Complete the conversation. Use your own words.

A: Are you _____?

B: No, _____. I'm _____.

A: Nice to meet you. I'm _____.

B: Good to meet you. What do you do?

A: I'm _____. What about you?

B: I'm _____.

A: Where are you from?

B: _____. And you?

A: I'm from _____.

➤ Practical grammar

5 **Complete the sentences. Write _am_, _are_, or _is_.**

1. I _am_ an engineer.

2. She _____ an electrician.

3. I _____ not a cook.

4. Mia _____ from Italy.

5. You _____ not a manager.

6. Ivan _____ my teacher.

6 **Write about the pictures. Write _He's_ or _She's_. Write _a_ or _an_.**

1. 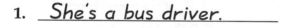 _She's a bus driver._   2. _____

3. _____   4. _____

7 Complete the conversations. Use a form of <u>be</u>.

1. A: <u>*Are you*</u> a student?

   B: Yes, I am.

2. A: _____ from San Francisco?

   B: No, she's not.

3. A: _____ unemployed?

   B: Yes, he is.

4. A: _____ from China?

   B: No. Fumiyo is from Japan.

8 Read. Answer the questions. Use a short answer with <u>be</u>.

> Lan is from Vietnam. She's an engineer. But right now she's unemployed.

1. Is Lan from China? <u>*No, she's not.*</u> _____

2. Is Lan from Vietnam? _____

3. Is Lan a housekeeper? _____

4. Is Lan an engineer? _____

5. Is Lan unemployed right now? _____

9 Write answers about <u>yourself</u>.

1. What's your name? _____

2. Where are you from? _____

3. Are you a student? _____

4. What do you do? _____

➤ Authentic practice

10 **Read. Choose your response. Circle the letter.**

1. "Can I help you?"

   a. Yes, I am.   **(b.)** Yes, thank you.

2. "What's your occupation?"

   a. I'm a homemaker.   **b.** No, I'm not.

3. "Are you employed or unemployed?"

   a. I'm unemployed.   **b.** Yes, I am.

4. "Good luck at your new job!"

   a. Yes, I am.   **b.** Thank you.

11 **Complete the paragraphs. Use words from the box.**

~~She~~	bus driver	She's	from	she

"We have three new students today. First is Fatima

Ahmed. ___She___ is from Sudan. _____ a homemaker.
        1.   2.

Our second new student is Oscar Fuentes. Oscar is a

_____ on the First Street bus route. Oscar is _____ Guatemala.
       3.   4.

And this is Tracy Liu. Tracy is from China, and _____ is a cook at a
                                                        5.

Chinese restaurant.

Please say 'hi' to Fatima, Oscar, and Tracy!"

12 **Look at Exercise 11 again. Complete the chart.**

Name	Country	Occupation
1. *Fatima Ahmed*	*Sudan*	
2.		*bus driver*
3. *Tracy Liu*		

13 Look at the list of students. Then complete the sentences.

FIRST STREET HOSPITAL
New Classes

Teacher	Mr. Andrew Stone
Class	English 4
Room	101

Students

Name	Occupation	Department
Safia Ali	Housekeeper	Housekeeping
Mehmet Boskovic	Electrician	Engineering
Ana Guzman	Cook	Cafeteria
Ibrahim Hassan	Cashier	Cafeteria
Toshi Kanaka	Housekeeper	Housekeeping
Elias Sandoval	Plumber	Engineering
Nina Costa	Cashier	Cafeteria
Eva Valdez	Housekeeper	Housekeeping

1. *Ibrahim Hassan* and _____ are cashiers.

2. Safia Ali, Eva Valdez, and _____ are housekeepers.

3. _____ is not a housekeeper. She is a cook.

4. _____ is an electrician, and _____

   is a plumber.

5. Andrew Stone is not a student. He is a _____.

14 Look at the list in Exercise 13 again. Complete the chart. Write the occupation or number.

Occupation	Number of students
1. electrician	1
2.	1
3. housekeeper	
4. plumber	
5.	2

15 Read the article. Then check ☑ <u>yes</u> or <u>no</u>.

New Employees

Andrew Stone

Please welcome Andrew Stone and Rita Torres to First Street Hospital!

Andrew Stone is our new English teacher. His classes are English 1 and English 4. Andrew is from Chicago, Illinois. He was an English teacher for hospital employees at Central Hospital in Chicago in 1998. He was also an English teacher in France. He speaks English and French.

Rita Torres is a new electrician in the Engineering Office. Rita is from Lima, Peru. She speaks Spanish and English. Rita is also a student at City College.

Good luck to Andrew and Rita!

Rita Torres

		yes	no
1.	Andrew Stone is a teacher.	☑	☐
2.	He is from France.	☐	☐
3.	He is a teacher at Central Hospital right now.	☐	☐
4.	Rita Torres is an electrician.	☐	☐
5.	She is unemployed.	☐	☐
6.	She is from Peru.	☐	☐

16 Look at Exercise 15 again. Complete the sentences.

1. The teacher's name is *Andrew Stone* _____.

2. He is from _____.

3. The electrician's name is _____.

4. She is from _____.

17 Complete the conversation. Write the letter on the line.

1. Hi. I'm Brenda Chen. What's your name? ___d___

2. And what's your occupation, please? _____

3. Are you employed right now? _____

4. Are you from Mexico? _____

5. OK, thanks. Please fill out this form. _____

a. Yes, I am.

b. No, I'm not. I'm from El Salvador.

c. Thank you.

d. Pablo. Pablo Garcia.

e. I'm an electrician.

18 Fill out the form. Write about <u>yourself</u>.

NAME: _____

          Last Name   First Name

OCCUPATION: _____

UNIT 2
The community

➤ Vocabulary

1 Look at the pictures. Check ☑ <u>yes</u> or <u>no</u>.

1. a meeting room
   ☐ yes ☑ no

2. a supply room
   ☐ yes ☐ no

3. a bank
   ☐ yes ☐ no

4. an exit
   ☐ yes ☐ no

5. a hall
   ☐ yes ☐ no

6. a school
   ☐ yes ☐ no

2 Complete the sentences. Write <u>at</u> or <u>in</u>.

1. The engineer is ___*in*___ the supply room.

2. Trudy is a homemaker. She is _____ home.

3. The manager is _____ the meeting room.

4. Mary is _____ school right now.

5. I'm sorry. Emir is _____ work now.

6. Is the bus driver _____ the parking lot?

3 Put the conversation in order. Write the number on the line.

_1_ Are the housekeepers here?

_____ OK. Where is the supply room?

_____ And where are the restrooms?

_____ No, they're not. They're in the supply room.

_____ They're on the right, next to the exit.

_4_ It's down the hall, on the left.

_7_ Thanks.

4 Complete the conversation. Use the map and your <u>own</u> words.

A: Excuse me. I'm looking for the

_____.

B: The _____? It's on _____ Street.

   It's _____ the _____.

A: Excuse me?

B: It's _____.

A: OK. Where are the _____ and the _____?

B: They're down the street, on _____.

A: _____.

B: You're welcome.

5 ➤ *CHALLENGE* Look at the picture. Read the sentences. Write the names on the lines.

Adele is on the left.
Ming is on the right.
Ria is not next to Ming.
Clara is between Adele and Ria.
Eva is not on the left.

Adele _____ _____ _____ _____
1.   2.   3.   4.   5.

➤ Practical grammar

6 Complete the conversations. Use words from the box.

we're	~~you're~~	they're	We're	They're

1. **A:** Excuse me. We're new students. Are we at the entrance?

   B: The entrance? No, _you're_ not. This is the exit.

2. **A:** Are you teachers?

   B: No, _____ not. _____ students.

3. **A:** Are the restrooms down the hall?

   B: Yes. _____ on the left.

4. **A:** Are the offices next to the supply room?

   B: No, _____ not. The offices are across from the supply room.

7 Put the words in order. Write questions.

1. **A:** the / you / room / Are / in / meeting / ?

   Are you in the meeting room? _____

   B: No, we're not. We're in the office.

2. **A:** drivers / you / bus / Are / ?

   _____

   B: Yes, we are.

3. **A:** Maple / we / Are / Street / on / ?

   _____

   B: No, we're not. This is Main Street.

4. **A:** teachers / Are / in / the / restaurant / the / ?

   _____

   B: No. They're in the parking lot.

8 Complete the conversations. Choose a word. Write the word on the line.

1. A: ___Where___ are your offices?
   Where / What

   B: We're in Park City, on River Place.

2. A: _____ the address, please?
   What / What's

   B: 1892 River Place.

3. A: OK. But _____ River Place?
   where / where's

   B: Between Bank Street and the post office.

4. A: OK, thanks. And _____ the manager?
   who's / what's

   B: Mr. Link. His first name is Gary.

5. A: OK. And _____ your name?
   what's / who's

   B: I'm Ann Payton. I'm the office manager.

   A: Thank you, Ms. Payton.

   B: You're welcome.

9 ►CHALLENGE Look at the answers. Write questions.

1. A: _What's your name?_____

   B: My name is Tony Soon.

2. A: _____

   B: They're from Korea.

3. A: _____

   B: The office is in Old Town.

4. A: _____

   B: The address is 135 Lincoln Street.

5. A: _____

   B: The cashiers? They're Jin and Tom.

➤ Authentic practice

10 **Read. Choose your response. Circle the letter.**

1. "Can you help us? We're looking for the women's restroom."

   a. Yes, it is.   **b.** It's across from the office.

2. "Do you know where Sam's Supermarket is?"

   a. No. I'm sorry.   **b.** No, we're not.

3. "It's next to the Metropolitan Authority Transit Station."

   a. Excuse me.   **b.** Excuse me?

4. "It's right down the street."

   a. Across from the supermarket?   **b.** You're welcome.

11 **Look at the map. Complete the conversation.**

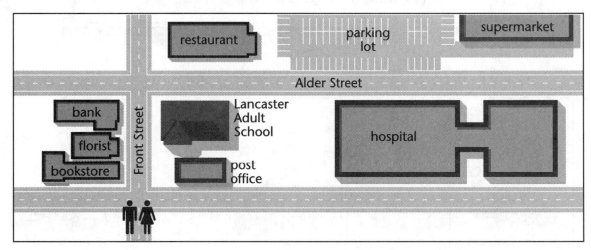

A: Excuse me. Do you know where Lancaster Adult School is?

B: Yes. It's _across from the bank_____.
    1.

A: Great. And are the florist and the bookstore on Alder Street?

B: No. They're _____.
    2.

A: OK. And my last question—where is the parking lot?

B: It's _____.
    3.

A: Thank you so much! I really appreciate it.

B: _____.
    4.

12 **Look at the poster.**

HELP WANTED
Work in Richmond's Newest Hotel!

Now hiring:

- Building Engineers
- Cashiers
- Cooks
- Front Desk Clerks
- Housekeepers

- Office Manager
- Parking Attendants
- Supplies Manager
- Van Drivers

The Old Town Hotel is located at:
692 Bank Street
Richmond, Virginia 23173

Interviews: Friday, March 23, 8 a.m. – 2 p.m.
Call (803) 555-1900 for an appointment.
Park in the guest parking lot across from the hotel.
The Personnel Manager is Mr. Kim.

Who can get a job at The Old Town Hotel? Circle the letters.

a. Kayo Hanai

b. Patricia Kelly

c. Ed Patrillo

d. Carl Olsen

e. Mariko Suzuki

f. Pablo Vega

13 Look again at the poster in Exercise 12. Complete the chart.

1. Workplace name	*The Old Town Hotel*
2. Workplace address	
3. Interview phone number	
4. Personnel manager	

14 ➤*CHALLENGE* Look at the map. Then read the sentences.

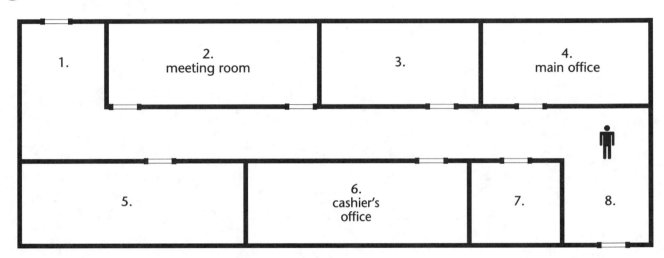

The main office is across from the entrance.
The manager's office is next to the main office.
The supply room is down the hall, across from the meeting room.
The cashier's office is between the supply room and the restrooms.
The exit is at the end of the hall, across from the supply room.

Now write the places on the lines.

1. _____

2. *meeting room* _____

3. _____

4. *main office* _____

5. _____

6. *cashier's office* _____

7. _____

8. _____

15 Look again at the map in Exercise 14. Complete the note.

We're in the meeting room.
It's_____

_____

_____

UNIT 3
Technology

➤ Vocabulary

1 Look at the pictures. Write the words. Then look at the gray boxes ☐ . What's the new word?

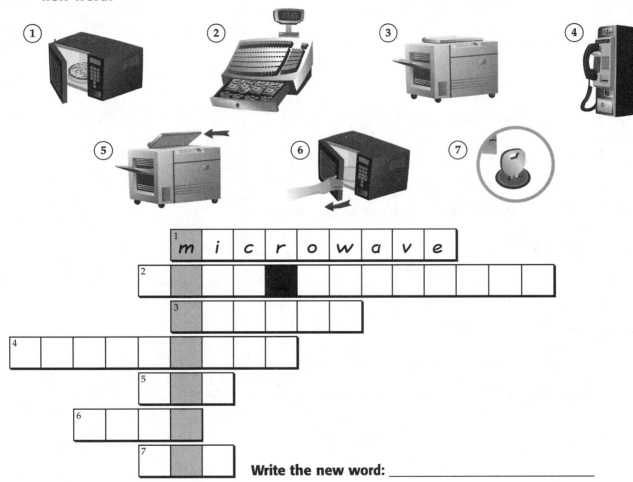

Write the new word: _____

2 Complete the chart. Use machines and parts of machines from your book or use your <u>own</u> machines. Write <u>a</u> or <u>an</u>.

unplug	open and close
a coffee maker	a lid

3 Complete the conversation. Use words from the box.

wrong	out of order	Turn	call	~~start~~

A: How do I ___*start*___ the lawn mower?
    1.

B: _____ the key.
        2.

A: OK. Where's the key?

B: I don't know. Let's _____ Mr. Elway.
                3.

A: Good idea. Oh, no!

B: What's _____?
            4.

A: The telephone is _____!
                5.

4 Complete the conversations. Use your <u>own</u> machines.

1. **A:** How do I start the _____?

   B: _____ the _____.

2. **A:** What's wrong?

   B: The _____ is out of order.

   A: OK. Don't _____ the _____.

   B: No problem.

   A: And let's call _____.

   B: Good idea.

➤ Practical grammar

5 **Complete the sentences. Write the letter on the line.**

1. Let's start __d__   a. the <u>off</u> button.

2. Let's call _____   b. the microwave.

3. Let's read _____   c. close the lid.

4. Let's press _____   d. the lawn mower.

5. Let's _____   e. the directions in the book.

6. Let's unplug _____   f. the manager.

6 **Complete the sentences. Use words from the box.**

start   ~~call~~   open   Read

Henri—

The copier is out of order. Please _____*call*_____ the Zeron copier company. The
1.

number is in the telephone book. Please _____ the door to the meeting
2.

room and please _____ the coffee maker. _____ the directions.
3.   4.

They're on the machine.

Thank you,
Tina

7 **Complete the conversations. Circle the letter.**

1. **A:** The coffee maker is out of order.

   B: **a.** Let's unplug the machine.   **b.** Don't turn the key.

2. **A:** **a.** Don't read the directions.   **b.** Let's read the directions.

   B: OK. They're on the machine.

3. **A:** The copier is out of order.

   B: **a.** Let's call the manager.   **b.** Don't call the manager.

8 **Look at the picture. Write suggestions or commands. Use <u>Let's</u> or <u>Don't</u> and words from the box.**

~~call the manager~~	close the door
unplug the copier	press <u>start</u>
start the coffee maker	

1. " _Let's call the manager._ _____ "

2. " _____ "

3. " _____ "

4. " _____ "

➤ Authentic practice

9 Read. Choose <u>your</u> response. Circle the letter.

1. "We need to call the equipment manager."

   a. Good to meet you.   **b.** Good idea.

2. "The cash register drawer is out of order. Don't open it."

   a. OK.   **b.** It's OK.

3. "How do you open the cash register?"

   a. Turn the key.   **b.** No problem.

4. "What's the problem?"

   a. Oh, no!   **b.** I don't know.

10 Match the pictures and the directions. Write the letter on the line.

To use your key card to open the office:

1. __*b*__ Put your key card in the machine.

2. _____ Press your card number.

3. _____ Open the door.

4. _____ Call 800-555-1630 for help.

a.   b.   c.   d.

11 Where are these directions and warnings? Check ✓ the boxes in the chart.

	a cash register	a microwave	a phone card
1. To start, turn the key.	✓		
2. Don't unplug, please.			
3. Press this card number: 011-1-886-62928.			
4. Sorry! Out of order.			
5. Close the door and press the <u>start</u> button.			

12 Read the message. Then check ✓ <u>yes</u>, <u>no</u>, or <u>I don't know</u>.

To _Dawit Yusuf_

Date _March 23_ Time _10:30_ A.M. ✓ P.M. ☐

WHILE YOU WERE OUT

<u>Ms. Bennett, District Adult School</u>

Phone _____ 259-1990 _____
Area code   Number   Extension

✓ telephoned   ☐ please call
☐ returned your call   ☐ will call back

Message _Copier problem._
Machine is out of order. Pls. meet
Ms. Bennett at the school and
look at the copy machine. The
address is 205 Oak Street. Thx.

	yes	no	I don't know
1. Ms. Bennett is from District Adult School.	✓	☐	☐
2. Dawit Yusuf is an English student.	☐	☐	☐
3. The Adult School copier is out of order.	☐	☐	☐
4. The Adult School is at 1990 Oak Street.	☐	☐	☐

13 Look at the pictures. Complete the directions. Use words from the box.

Don't open	Press	Don't press	open

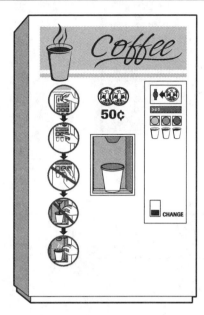

1. __Put 50¢ in the machine.__

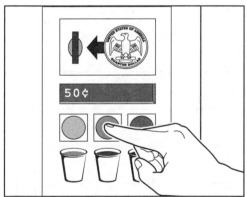

2. _____ the button.

3. _____ two buttons.

4. Wait. _____ the door.

5. Now _____ the door.

14 ► *CHALLENGE* **Write a note to your co-worker. Use words from the box and your own words. Sign your name.**

For problems with the phone in the hall, call Ben Osman at 744-2551

telephone	out of order	Please	call

Dear _____,

_____

_____

_____

Thanks! _____

_____

UNIT 4

The consumer world

➤ Vocabulary

1 Look at the picture. Complete the chart.

	Person	Uniform?	Clothes
1.	4	no	a jacket, pants
2.		yes	a dress
3.	1		a jacket, a skirt
4.	6	no	
5.	2	yes	
6.		no	a suit, a jacket, a skirt

2 Write about **your** clothes. Complete the chart.

Clothes	Colors
Example: *shirt*	*blue and green*

3 Choose the response. Write the letter on the line.

1. Do you have housekeeper uniforms? _____

2. What size? _____

3. I need these pants in medium. _____

4. I need a blue shirt. _____

5. What color? _____

a. OK. What size?

b. Medium, please.

c. Yes, we do.

d. Red, please.

e. OK. What color?

4 Complete the conversations. Use the pictures or your <u>own</u> words.

1. **A:** May I help you?

   B: Yes, please. These _____

   are _____.

   A: Oh, I'm sorry. Do you have the receipt?

   B: No, I'm sorry. It's at home.

2. **A:** I need _____, please.

   B: _____. What size?

   A: _____. And do you have this

   _____ in _____?

   B: _____.

➤ Practical grammar

5 Complete the sentences. Use words from the box.

has	need	doesn't want	~~needs~~	likes	have	don't like

1. The manager ____*needs*____ you. She's in the meeting room.

2. I _____ this uniform. It's yellow. I like blue.

3. We _____ a new computer. It's green.

4. Anna _____ the old supermarket.

5. Oh, no! The cash register is out of order. I _____ the directions.

6. Cheryl _____ two last names.

7. Mimi _____ these shoes. They're too small.

6 Look at the answers. Write questions. Use words from each box.

Do Does	I you he she we they	like need want have	old clothes? a computer? uniforms? an orange dress? a new phone number? the key?

1. _*Does he have the key?*_ _____ Yes, he does.

2. _____ No, they don't.

3. _____ Yes, we do.

4. _____ No, she doesn't.

5. _____ No, I don't.

7 **Look at the pictures. Complete the sentences. Use <u>this</u>, <u>that</u>, <u>these</u>, or <u>those</u>.**

I want _____ book, please.
1.

OK. Sure.

Do we need _____ receipts?
2.

No, we don't.

Do you like _____ shoes?
3.

No, I don't. I like _____ shoes.
4.

I want _____ computer.
5.
But I need _____
6.
lawn mower.

8 **Answer the questions. Use your <u>own</u> words. Write a short answer.**

1. Do you have a uniform? _____

2. Does your teacher need new shoes? _____

3. Do your classmates like computers? _____

4. What colors do you like? _____

28   Unit 4

➤ Authentic practice

9 Read. Choose your response. Circle the letter.

1. "I need some help. This skirt is too small."

   a. And what color?   **b.** Oh, I'm sorry.

2. "Do you have the key to the cash register?"

   a. Yes, I think so.   **b.** It's too large.

3. "What do those customers want?"

   a. They need a receipt.   **b.** They have a receipt.

4. "Excuse me. Do you have this suit in blue?"

   a. No, we don't. It's too small.   **b.** Sure. This way, please.

5. "I don't like this shirt. It's the wrong color."

   a. Do you have a receipt?   **b.** What size?

10 Put the conversation in order. Write the number on the line.

____1____ Can I help you?

_____ Yes, we do. What size do you want?

_____ I don't know. What sizes do you have?

_____ Super is too large. I want a medium, please.

_____ Yes, please. Do you have Coola Cola?

____7____ OK.

_____ We have small, medium, large, and super.

11 ▶ *CHALLENGE* **Read the conversation.**

Manager: OK—What do we have today?

Driver: I have 15 microwaves.

Manager: OK. I want 9 microwaves in the store. Keep 9 in the store and put 6 microwaves in the stock room.

Driver: There are 10 coffee makers.

Manager: Don't put the coffee makers in the stock room. I need those in the store.

Driver: All right. Let's see—we have 15 telephones.

Manager: Put the telephones next to the cash registers in the store.

Driver: What about the computers? I have 10 computers. They're in the blue boxes.

Manager: We need 5 computers in the store. Put 5 in the stock room.

Driver: OK. Here's your receipt.

Manager: Great. Thanks.

Look at the chart. Read the conversation again. Where does the manager want the machines? Complete the chart.

Item	Total number	In the store	In the stock room
microwaves	15	9	6
coffee makers			
telephones			
computers			

12 Read the memo. Then check ☑ <u>yes</u> or <u>no</u>.

Howard Hotel and Convention Center

Memo
To: All employees
From: Mrs. Burton
Re: New uniforms

All employees need new uniforms. Please check this list for your new uniform.

Mechanics: green shirt and blue pants; no tie
Cooks: white pants and white shirt
Bus drivers: white shirt, black pants, black tie
Housekeepers: green dress OR green shirt and pants
Parking lot attendants: blue pants, white shirt, blue tie

Buy the uniforms at Peerless Uniform Company and at A+ Uniforms on State Street. You need a receipt. Bring your receipt to the hotel cashier's office.

---

		yes	no
1.	Cooks and bus drivers need white shirts.	❑	❑
2.	Irma is a parking lot attendant. She needs black pants.	❑	❑
3.	A+ Uniforms has the new uniforms.	❑	❑
4.	Employees don't need a receipt.	❑	❑

13 Look at the memo in Exercise 12 again. Complete the telephone conversation.

Salesperson: Hello. A Plus Uniforms.

Customer: Hi. I'm a mechanic at Howard Hotel. Do you have our new uniforms?

Salesperson: Yes, we _____. What do you need?
                                    1.

Customer: Well, I have blue pants at home, but I don't have a _____ shirt.
                                                                        2.

Salesperson: OK. What _____ do you need?
                              3.

Customer: Well, I know medium is too small. I need it in _____.
                                                                 4.

Salesperson: Do you need a tie?

Customer: _____.
                    5.

Salesperson: OK. Then we have everything you need.

Customer: Great. Thanks for your time.

14 Look at the refund policy and return form. Then write Tasha Carter's words.

King's Restaurant Supply
Where the customer is king!

Refund and Exchange Policy
Refunds and exchanges for customers with receipts.

King's Restaurant Supply   **Refund / Exchange Form**

Customer name: _Tasha Carter_

Item returned: _coffee maker_

Returned for ☒ credit card refund   ☐ exchange

Reason for return: _wrong size_

"Excuse me. I need to return this _____. It's the

_____ for my restaurant. I need a large one. I have my

_____, and I want a credit card _____."

15 Read about Sofia Hassan. Then complete the return form for Sofia.

Sofia Hassan needs to exchange a computer. It's the wrong color.
She wants a blue computer. She has her receipt.

Refund / Exchange Form

Customer name: _____

Item returned: _____

Returned for ☐ credit card refund   ☐ exchange

Reason for return: _____

Name _____   ID _____   Date _____

UNIT 5

Time

➤ Vocabulary

1 Write the time. Use words.

1.    *four thirty-five*

2.    _____

3.    _____

4. _____

5.    _____

6. _____

2 Look at the pictures. Answer the questions.

1. What time is it? _____

2. What day is it? _____

3. What month is it? _____

4. What year is it? _____

5. What day is tomorrow? _____

Today is
Monday
15
August
2002

3 Write about <u>today</u>.

_____

    day   month   year   time

➤ Practical conversations

4 Complete the conversation. Use words from the box.

think	~~it~~	when	sure	It's	late	time

A: What time is _____*it*_____?
1.

B: _____ 10:45.
2.

A: Uh-oh. Allen's _____.
3.

B: No, he's not. He's at a computer class.

A: Oh. What _____ does the class start?
4.

B: At 10:30, I _____. I'm not _____.
5.   6.

A: And _____ does it end?
7.

B: At noon.

5 Complete the conversation. Use the signs or your __own__ words.

A: What time does the _____?

B: _____.

A: OK. And when does it _____?

B: _____, I think.

A: What time is it right now?

B: It's _____.

➤ Practical grammar

6 Complete the conversations. Choose words. Write the words on the line.

1. **A:** ___*Is it*___ 12:00?
   _{Is it / It is}

   B: No, it isn't. It's 11:30.

2. **A:** What time is it?

   B: _____ 6:45.
   _{Is / It's}

3. **A:** Is it July?

   B: No, _____. It's June.
   _{it is / it isn't}

4. **A:** _____ June 1?
   _{Is it / It is}

   B: No, it isn't. It's June 2.

7 ➤ CHALLENGE Look at the answers. Write questions. Use words from the box and your <u>own</u> words.

~~What time is~~   What time does   When is   When does   When do

1. **A:** *What time is it?* _____

   B: It's 3:00.

2. **A:** _____

   B: English classes start in January.

3. **A:** _____

   B: The class ends in May.

4. **A:** _____

   B: The supply room closes at 4:30 p.m.

5. **A:** _____

   B: The meeting is on Tuesday.

8 Look at the pictures. Match the directions and the ordinal numbers. Write the letter on the line.

Microwave Oven Instructions

1. _____ Press the <u>stop</u> button.   **a.** first

2. _____ Open the door.   **b.** second

3. _____ Close the door.   **c.** third

4. _____ Press the <u>start</u> button.   **d.** fourth

9 Put the words in order. Write sentences.

1. the / open / does / When / office / ?

   <u>When does the office open</u>?

2. close / What / time / post office / does / the / ?

   _____

3. does / What / start / the / time / class / ?

   _____

4. meeting / When / the / is / ?

   _____

5. it / Sunday / Is / ?

   _____

6. I / June 14, / ends / think / School / on / .

   _____

10 Answer the questions. Use your <u>own</u> words.

1. What time does your English class start?

   _____

2. What time does it end?

   _____

➤ Authentic practice

11 **Read. Choose <u>your</u> response. Circle the letter.**

1. "Can you work tomorrow?"

   a. I'm late.   **b.** I think so. Yes, that's OK.

2. "Your first day is Monday, June 29."

   a. That's great.   **b.** And when does it close?

3. "We have an employee meeting on Wednesday at 2:30."

   a. OK. No problem.   **b.** I'm not sure.

4. "Can you be a little early tomorrow?"

   a. Sure. What time?   **b.** At noon.

5. "See you tomorrow."

   a. You're welcome.   **b.** Bye.

12 **Who says this? Check ☑ <u>Manager</u> or <u>Employee</u>.**

	Manager	Employee
1. What time can you start?	✓	
2. What time does my shift end?		
3. You're a little early. That's good.		
4. Can I start a little late on Thursday?		
5. Do I need a uniform?		
6. The second shift starts at 4:30 p.m. Is that OK?		

13 Look at the work schedule. Then look at the times. Who is at work? Write the name on the line.

24/7 EXPRESS

WORK SCHEDULE   WEEK OF _February 8–14_

	Morning Shift 6:00 a.m. – 2:00 p.m.	Evening Shift _____	Midnight Shift 10:00 p.m. – 6:00 a.m.
Mon	Lul	_____	Nikolai
Tue	Mina	_____	Nikolai
Wed	Mina	_____	_____
Thu	Mina	_____	_____
Fri	Mina	_____	Nikolai
Sat	Lul	Juanita	Nikolai
Sun	Lul	Juanita	Nikolai

1. Monday, 7:00 a.m.   _Lul_____

2. Thursday, 1:30 p.m. _____

3. Saturday, 11:45 a.m. _____

4. Tuesday, 4:15 a.m.   _____

5. Friday, noon   _____

14 Read the paragraph. Complete the work schedule in Exercise 13.

> At 24 / 7 Express, the evening shift starts at 2:00 p.m. It ends at 10:00 p.m. George has the evening shift Monday to Friday. Pierre is a new cashier. He has the midnight shift Wednesday and Thursday.

15 Look at the work schedule in Exercise 13 again. Complete the paragraphs. Use words from the box.

starts	2:00 p.m.	early	~~6:00 a.m.~~	ends

At 24 / 7 Express, the morning shift starts at ___*6:00 a.m.*___. It

1.

ends at _____. The midnight shift doesn't start at midnight.

2.

It _____ at 10:00 p.m. and _____ at 6:00 a.m.

3.   4.

On Tuesday, Mina has the morning shift. She is at work at 5:45 a.m.

She is a little _____.

5.

16 Look at the time card. Look at the work schedule in Exercise 13. Then check ☑ <u>yes</u> or <u>no</u>.

24/7 EXPRESS   **Employee Time Card**

Name *Nikolai Stavros*   Shift *Midnight*

Date	Time In	Time Out
Mon. Feb 8	9:45 p.m.	6:00 a.m.
Tues. Feb 9	10:00 p.m.	6:00 a.m.
Wed. Feb 10		
Thu. Feb 11		
Fri. Feb 12	10:00 p.m.	6:30 a.m.
Sat. Feb 13	10:10 p.m.	6:00 a.m.
Sun. Feb 14	9:50 p.m.	6:00 a.m.

	yes	**no**
1. Nikolai's shift starts at 10:00 p.m.	☑	☐
2. Nikolai's shift ends at midnight.	☐	☐
3. Nikolai is at work on Friday.	☐	☐
4. On Tuesday, Nikolai is on time.	☐	☐
5. Nikolai is a little early on Saturday.	☐	☐
6. Nikolai is late three days this week.	☐	☐

17 **Look at the map. Answer the questions.**

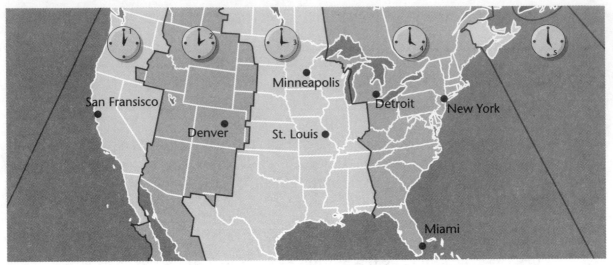

1. It's 3:00 p.m. in Miami. Is it 3:00 p.m. in Detroit? ___Yes, it is.___

2. It's 9:30 a.m. in St. Louis. Where is it 8:30 a.m.? _____

3. It's 10:00 p.m. in San Francisco. What time is it in New York? _____

4. It's 11:00 a.m. in Minneapolis. What time is it in Miami? _____

18 ►*CHALLENGE* **Read Angela Black's schedule for this week. Then complete her date book.**

- This week, work starts at 8:00 a.m. on Monday, Wednesday, and Friday. Angela's shift ends at 4:00 p.m.
- On Tuesday and Thursday, work starts at 12:00 noon. It ends at 6:00 p.m.
- On Monday, Angela has computer class at 7:00 p.m. The class ends at 9:30 p.m.
- On Saturday, she wants to see a movie at 8:30 p.m.
- She calls home on Sunday.

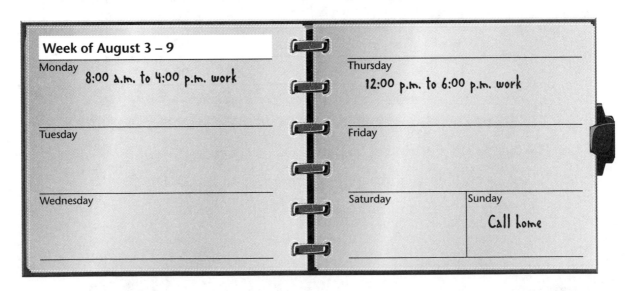

Week of August 3 – 9

Monday
8:00 a.m. to 4:00 p.m. work

Tuesday

Wednesday

Thursday
12:00 p.m. to 6:00 p.m. work

Friday

Saturday

Sunday
Call home

U N I T 6

Supplies and services

➤ Vocabulary

1 **Complete the sentences. Use the pictures or your own words.**

1. This food is white. People put it in coffee. It's not a drink. It's _sugar_____.

2. These foods are red. They are _____ and _____.

3. This food is green. It's _____.

4. These are white and yellow. They are _____.

5. These drinks are brown. They are _____ and _____.

2 **Complete the charts. Use words from your book or your own words.**

I eat these foods at home.	I eat these foods at work.	I eat these foods at a restaurant.
Examples: *meat*	*apples*	*chicken*

I buy these foods and drinks at the supermarket.	I buy these foods and drinks from a machine.

➤ Practical conversations

3 Complete the conversation. Use words from the box.

too	box	drinks	~~up~~	what	out

A: Hi, Amy. What's _____ *up* _____?
1.

B: Not much. But we're _____ of tea. We have a meeting at
2.

11:00 today, and we need _____.
3.

A: Well, _____ about coffee?
4.

B: I really don't like coffee. I like tea.

A: Me _____.
5.

B: Let's call Beth. I think she has a _____ of tea in her office.
6.

A: Good idea.

4 Complete the conversations. Use the pictures or your **own** words.

1. **A:** What's up?

   B: Not much. But we need _____

   and a _____ of _____.

   A: OK. Anything else?

   B: Yes. We're out of _____.

   A: OK.

2. **A:** Is there any _____ on the shelf?

   B: Yes, there is.

   A: And are there any _____?

   B: No, there aren't. Let's look in _____.

   A: OK.

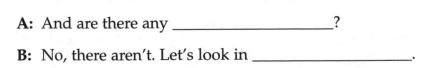

➤ Practical grammar

5 Look at the words. Check ☑ <u>Count noun</u> or <u>Non-count noun</u>. Write plural forms of the count nouns.

	Count noun	Non-count noun	Plural
1. bottle	✔		*bottles*
2. juice		✔	—
3. water			
4. carrot			
5. egg			

6 Complete the sentences. Write <u>How many</u> or <u>How much</u>.

1. *How many* _____ carrots do you need?

2. _____ meat do you buy in one month?

3. _____ refrigerators does Kim's Restaurant have?

4. _____ bags of carrots are in the refrigerator?

5. _____ sugar do you like in your tea?

6. _____ cans of apple juice do we have in the supply room?

7 Look at the answers. Write questions. Use <u>How many</u> or <u>How much</u>.

1. A: *How much coffee do they have?* _____

   B: They have four cans of coffee.

2. A: _____

   B: He needs six eggs.

3. A: _____

   B: They want two boxes of rice.

4. A: _____

   B: Her name has seven letters.

8 Complete the sentences. Choose words. Write the words on the line.

1. There's _____ at work today.
   new drivers / a new driver

2. There are _____ in the refrigerator.
   six boxes of eggs / a box of eggs

3. There are _____ on Mondays and Wednesdays.
   English classes / English class

4. There is _____ on the shelf.
   a can of milk / cans of milk

9 Write questions with **Are there any** and **Is there any**. Then complete the answers.

1. _Are there any_ customers in the store?   Yes, _there are_____.

2. _____ coffee in the meeting room?   No, _____.

3. _____ sugar in this tea?   Yes, _____.

4. _____ bags of carrots in the refrigerator?   Yes, _____.

5. _____ computers in your classroom?   No, _____.

➤ Authentic practice

10 Read. **Choose _your_ response. Circle the letter.**

1. "Hi, John. What's up with you today?"
   a. Not much.   **b.** Today, I think.

2. "I need a large cup of coffee."
   a. How much coffee do you need?   **b.** OK. Anything else?

3. "We really love apples."
   a. What about you?   **b.** Me too!

4. "I like to work with customers."
   a. Not me.   **b.** Not much.

5. "I like milk in my tea."
   a. Yes, there is.   **b.** What about sugar?

11 ➤*CHALLENGE* **Read the conversation. Then check ☑ _yes_ or _no_.**

A: What do we need for today?
B: Well, I know we need bread.
A: OK. What about meat or cheese?
B: There's not much in the refrigerator. We need chicken and cheese.
A: And what about drinks?
B: We have a new can of coffee, so that's not a problem.
A: Do we have any milk?
B: A little. Let's buy a large bottle. And some sugar.
A: How much?
B: One box, I think.
A: Oh, are there any tomatoes on the shelf?
B: No, there aren't. Let's buy tomatoes.
A: OK. Anything else?
B: No, that's it.

	yes	no
1. They need bread.	☑	☐
2. They need to buy cheese.	☐	☐
3. They need a new can of coffee.	☐	☐
4. They want a small bottle of milk.	☐	☐
5. They want one box of sugar.	☐	☐
6. There are tomatoes on the shelf.	☐	☐
7. They want tomatoes.	☐	☐

12 **Look at the picture. Complete the directions. Use words from the box.**

| ~~large~~ | bread | fish | tomato | onion | lettuce |

Start with the _____large_____ paper
1.

wrapper. Put a piece of bread on the paper.

Put the _____ on the bread.
2.

Then put one slice of _____ on
3.

the fish. Then put on 3 slices of _____
4.

and the _____. Put on the second
5.

piece of _____. Last, wrap the
6.

sandwich in the paper.

**Harry's Seafood
Fish Sandwich**

13 **Read the conversations. Complete the order forms.**

1. **A:** Welcome to Taco Time.
        Can I help you?
    B: Yes, please. I want a taco salad.
    A: OK. Do you want any beef or
        chicken on your salad?
    B: No, thanks. I don't eat meat.
    A: OK. Do you want anything to drink?
    B: Yes. A small apple juice, please.
    A: OK.

TACO TIME

TACOS   0075
Qty.

☐   Bean and cheese taco
        ☐ Lettuce   ☐ Tomatoes

☐   Chicken taco
        ☐ Lettuce   ☐ Tomatoes

☐   Beef taco
        ☐ Lettuce   ☐ Tomatoes

SALADS
Qty.

☑   Taco salad
☐   Taco salad with chicken
☐   Taco salad with beef

DRINKS

Qty.		small	medium	large
☐	Coffee	☐	☐	☐
☐	Iced tea	☐	☐	☐
☐	Milk	☐	☐	☐
☐	Orange juice	☐	☐	☐
☑	Apple juice	✔	☐	☐
☐	Soda	☐	☐	☐

2. A: Hi. Can I help you?

B: Yes, thanks. I'd like two chicken tacos.

A: OK. Two chicken tacos. Do you want lettuce and tomatoes?

B: Lettuce is OK. No tomatoes.

A: OK. Two chicken tacos, no tomatoes. Anything else?

B: Yes. I'd like a medium coffee, please.

A: Great. Thanks.

TACO TIME

TACOS   0076
Qty.
☐ Bean and cheese taco
   ☐ Lettuce   ☐ Tomatoes
☐ Chicken taco
   ☐ Lettuce   ☐ Tomatoes
☐ Beef taco
   ☐ Lettuce   ☐ Tomatoes

SALADS
Qty.
☐ Taco salad
☐ Taco salad with chicken
☐ Taco salad with beef

DRINKS

Qty.		small	medium	large
☐	Coffee	☐	☐	☐
☐	Iced tea	☐	☐	☐
☐	Milk	☐	☐	☐
☐	Orange juice	☐	☐	☐
☐	Apple juice	☐	☐	☐
☐	Soda	☐	☐	☐

3. A: Hi. What would you like today?

B: I need three bean and cheese tacos and a chicken salad.

A: Is a taco salad with chicken OK?

B: Yes, thanks.

A: And do you want lettuce and tomatoes on the tacos?

B: Yes, please.

A: OK. Anything to drink?

B: Yes. I'd like a small bottle of milk.

A: I'm sorry. We're out of milk today.

B: That's OK. How about two small bottles of orange juice?

A: Sure. Thank you.

TACO TIME

TACOS   0077
Qty.
☐ Bean and cheese taco
   ☐ Lettuce   ☐ Tomatoes
☐ Chicken taco
   ☐ Lettuce   ☐ Tomatoes
☐ Beef taco
   ☐ Lettuce   ☐ Tomatoes

SALADS
Qty.
☐ Taco salad
☐ Taco salad with chicken
☐ Taco salad with beef

DRINKS

Qty.		small	medium	large
☐	Coffee	☐	☐	☐
☐	Iced tea	☐	☐	☐
☐	Milk	☐	☐	☐
☐	Orange juice	☐	☐	☐
☐	Apple juice	☐	☐	☐
☐	Soda	☐	☐	☐

14 Look at the pictures. What do you need to make Tomato Rice? Check ✓ the boxes.

❏ onion

❏ chicken

❏ water

❏ rice

❏ fish

❏ cheese

❏ tomato juice

Tomato Rice

1

2 4 cups tomato juice

Tomato Juice

3 2 cups rice

RICE

4

5 1 cup cheese

Cheese

15 Look at the pictures in Exercise 14 again. Put the directions in order. Write the number on the line.

__1__ Chop 1 onion.

_____ Cook the rice, onion, and tomato juice for 45 minutes.

_____ Put 2 cups of rice and the onion in the tomato juice.

_____ Put cheese in the rice. Eat!

_____ Boil 4 cups of tomato juice.

UNIT 7

Relationships

➤ Vocabulary

1 **Complete the sentences. Use words from your book.**

1. Lena is a _____mother_____ and

   a _____wife_____.

2. George is a _____ and

   a _____.

3. Artie is a _____ and

   a _____.

4. Belinda is a _____ and

   a _____.

Lena   George

Artie   Belinda

2 **What do the people do? Write the letter on the line.**

1. __c__ student   **a.** cooks and cleans at home

2. _____ homemaker   **b.** drives a bus

3. _____ housekeeper   **c.** studies

4. _____ mechanic   **d.** fixes a bus

5. _____ bus driver   **e.** cleans a hotel room

3 **➤ CHALLENGE   Complete the chart. Use your own words.**

People clean	People fix
offices	cars

4 **Put the conversation in order. Write the number on the line.**

_____ No, I'm sorry. I'm not ready yet.

___1___ Are you ready to go?

_____ What's wrong?

_____ I don't know. I have to look at the directions.

_____ I'm fixing this cash register. It's out of order.

_____ Why not? What are you doing?

5 **Complete the conversations. Use the pictures or your <u>own</u> words.**

1. **A:** Can you _____ the _____?

   B: No, I'm sorry. I can't right now.

   A: Why not?

   B: Because I have to _____.

   A: Well, when can you _____?

   B: In _____, I think.

   A: OK.

2. **A:** Is Edna ready to _____?

   B: No, not yet.

   A: Why? What's she doing?

   B: She's _____ right now.

➤ Practical grammar

6 Complete the sentences. Use the present continuous. Write the words on the line.

1. I **'m staying** _____ at home today.
         _{stay}

2. Julio _____ the computer right now.
            _{fix}

3. Ellen _____ the meeting room.
          _{clean}

4. _____ Julian _____ the bus?
                 _{drive}

5. _____ you _____ today?
              _{work}

7 ➤**CHALLENGE** Look at the answers. Complete the questions. Use the present continuous.

1. Who **'s going to the store** _____? Terry is going to the store.

2. What _____? Sofia is buying a blue jacket.

3. Where _____? Hanna is going to London.

4. Why _____? Luz is calling the electrician because she can't install the machine.

8 Complete the sentences. Write the letter on the line.

1. I can __e__   **a.** to work today. He can stay home.

2. Carlos can't _____   **b.** come because he's working.

3. We have to _____   **c.** call the shift manager. The machine's out of order.

4. Mary has _____   **d.** buy a new skirt. This old skirt is OK.

5. I don't have to _____   **e.** help you in 15 minutes, but right now I'm busy.

6. My father doesn't have _____   **f.** to go to the hospital with her mother.

9 **Complete the sentences. Choose words. Write the words on the line.**

1. I _____ a new car.

have / have to

2. Peter _____ fix the copier today.

has / has to

3. Sharla _____ call her daughter.

has / has to

4. Julio and Simone _____ a good manager.

have / have to

10 **Write sentences. Use words from each box.**

I	have to	work.
My father	don't have to	clean this room.
My sister	has to	go to the supermarket today.
My friends	doesn't have to	study English.
My manager		go to school.
		work on Saturday.

1. *I don't have to work on Saturday.* _____

2. _____

3. _____

4. _____

➤ Authentic practice

11 Read. Choose <u>your</u> response. Circle the letter.

1. "Are you ready yet?"

   a. No, I'm sorry. Not yet.   **b.** No, I'm sorry. I can't.

2. "When does the next shift start?"

   a. In room 30.   **b.** In 30 minutes.

3. "Why can't you go to the restaurant?"

   a. Because I have to study.   **b.** I have to go.

4. "Can you clean the refrigerator today?"

   a. Sure. I'm not busy.   **b.** Yes, I am.

5. "What do you have to do after work?"

   a. I have to go to the store   **b.** I'm busy right now.

12 Read the job announcement. Then answer the questions. Check ☑ <u>yes</u> or <u>no</u>.

> ### Job announcement #206E
>
> We have the following jobs available:
> - Hotel Housekeeper — clean hotel rooms, work weekends
> - Salesperson — work with customers, use a cash register
> - Computer Technician — fix computers, drive
>
> Apply in the Personnel Office, Room 149.

	yes	no
1. Alba Nemeth can clean. She can work on weekends. Can she get the housekeeper job?	❏	❏
2. Jose Mendez can fix computers, but he can't drive. Can he get the computer technician job?	❏	❏
3. Anton Gross likes to work with people. He can drive, and he can use a cash register. Can Anton get the salesperson job?	❏	❏

Look at the announcement again. Complete the sentences about <u>yourself</u>.

4. I can get the _____ job because I can _____.

5. I can't get the _____ job because I can't _____.

13 Look at the work schedule. Then complete the conversation.

Mai's Office Cleaning Service

Schedule for the week of March 23

Name	10:00 p.m.–12:30 a.m.	12:30 a.m.–3:00 a.m.	3:00 a.m.–3:30 a.m.	3:30 a.m.–6:00 a.m.
Lena	Clean the first-floor restrooms	Clean the second-floor hall	Eat lunch	Clean the third-floor offices
Mai	Clean the first-floor offices	Clean the second-floor restrooms	Eat lunch	Clean the third-floor hall
Norman	Clean the first-floor hall	Clean the second-floor offices	Eat lunch	Clean the third-floor restrooms

A: It's 1:00 a.m. Where's Mai?

B: She's on the _____*second*_____ floor.
　　　　　　　　　　　　　　1.

A: What is she doing?

B: She's *cleaning the second-floor restrooms*_____.
　　　　　　　　　　　　　　　　　　　2.

A: What about Lena? Is she busy?

B: Yes, _____. She's _____.
　　　　　　　3.　　　　　　　　　　　　　　　　　4.

A: Norman is here today, right? Is he cleaning the parking lot?

B: _____.
　　　　　　　　　　　　　　5.

A: What's he doing?

B: He's _____.
　　　　　　　　　　　　　　6.

14 Look at the work schedule in Exercise 13 again. Answer the questions.

1. It's 10:30 p.m. What is Lena doing?

   *She's cleaning the first-floor restrooms.*_____

2. It's 3:15 a.m. What are Mai and Norman doing?

   _____

3. It's 5:15 a.m. Is Lena cleaning restrooms? _____

   What is she doing?_____

54　　Unit 7

15 Kami Jones is a telephone company technician. She installs new telephones and fixes old telephones. Look at the work order for Kami. Complete the sentences. Choose words. Write the words on the line.

Mid-West Telephone Company

Work Order

Company: _Ted's Auto Repair School_

Address: _5150 56th St._

Job	Task	Item	Location
1	☑ install ☐ fix	1 New telephone	Room 208 (office) On small desk to the right of the copier
2	☑ install ☐ fix	1 New telephone	Room 213 (computer room) On teacher's desk
3	☐ install ☑ fix	2 Old telephones	Hall, across from Room 209

Notes: _The computer room is locked. You can get the key from Ann in Room 208._

1. Kami has to _____ the new telephones.
   install / fix

2. Kami has to install a telephone on the _____ in the office.
   copier / desk

3. In the computer room, Kami has to install _____.
   one telephone / two telephones

4. Kami has to _____ two telephones in the hall.
   install / fix

5. Ann has the key for _____.
   room 208 / the computer room

6. Kami needs _____ new telephones today.
   two / four

16 ▶ *CHALLENGE* Read the note. Complete the new work order for Kami.

Kami-

I know you are busy today, but could you install one more telephone? It's at the Shop Away Supermarket at 1100 Allison St. They need a new telephone in the office. Thanks very much.

Floyd

Mid-West Telephone Company

Work Order

Company: _____

Address: _____

Job	Task	Item	Location
1	☑ install ☐ fix		

17 Read the personal day policy.

Personal Day Policy

- You may take three personal days a year.
- You must talk to your manager one day BEFORE your personal day.
- You also have to fill out a personal day form one day before your personal day.
- If you want a personal day on Monday, you must talk to your manager <u>and</u> fill out a personal day form on Friday.

Bonita Sandoval is a new employee. Answer her questions about the personal day policy.

1. **Bonita:** How many personal days can I take in one year?

    YOU You can take _____.

2. **Bonita:** What do I have to do before a personal day?

    YOU You have to _____.

    You also have to _____.

3. **Bonita:** If I want to take a personal day on Monday, when do I have to fill out a personal day form?

    YOU On _____.

18 Look at the personal day policy in Exercise 17 again. Read the sentences. What do the <u>underlined</u> words mean? Circle the letter.

1. You <u>may</u> take three personal days a year.   **a.** have to   **b.** can

2. You <u>must</u> talk to your manager one day
   before your personal day.   **a.** have to   **b.** can

19 Read about Oscar Fuentes. Then complete Oscar's personal day form.

Oscar Fuentes is an employee at 24 / 7 Express. He works at store number 187. Oscar wants to talk to his son's teachers. He can go to his son's school on November 11th. He needs to take a personal day.

24/7 EXPRESS **Personal Day Form**

Employee name: _____   Store number: _____

Date of personal day: _____   Date of return to work: _____

Give this form to your manager before your personal day.

UNIT 8

Health and safety

➤ Vocabulary

1 Complete the sentences. Write the letters of each word in the boxes.

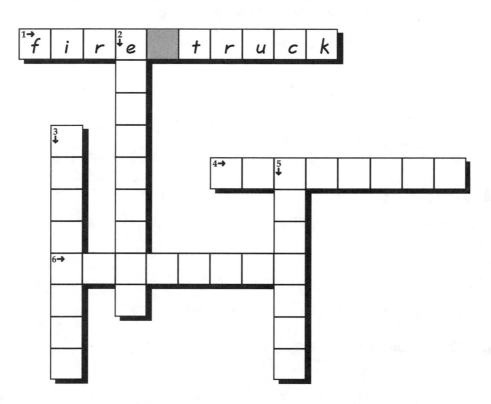

Across →

1. There's a fire on Oak Avenue. We need a _____.
4. Sheila has a headache. Can she take this ____?
6. Call an ambulance! There's an _____ on Second Street!

Down ↓

2. The ambulance parking lot is next to the _____ room.
3. Arturo's back hurts. He has a _____.
5. David is a nurse. He works with two _____.

2 Complete the sentences. Use words for parts of the body.

1. Your _____ is between your neck and your wrist.

2. Your _____ is between your leg and your foot.

3. Your wrist is between your _____ and your _____.

3 Put the conversation in order. Write the number on the line.

_____ Oh, I'm sorry. Can I call you back in ten minutes?

_____ OK. Bye.

__1__ Hello?

_____ Hi, Ming. This is Sara. Can you talk right now?

_____ Yes, that's fine. Talk to you then.

_____ No, I can't. I'm helping a customer.

4 Complete the conversation. Use your **own** words.

A: Doctor _____'s office. How can I help you?

B: This is _____. I need to make an appointment.

I _____.

A: Oh, I'm sorry. How about _____ at _____?

B: _____? Oh, I'm busy at _____. Is

_____ OK?

A: Yes, that's fine. Feel better!

B: Thank you very much. See you _____.

➤ Practical grammar

5 **Complete the sentences. Use words from the box.**

| Their | his | ~~My~~ | His | Our | your |

1. I have to go to the doctor. ___My___ back hurts.

2. My son can't go to school today. He hurt _____ ankle.

3. Please call the supervisors. _____ number is 535-2217.

4. We have a problem. _____ computers are out of order.

5. Do you have a fever? Call _____ doctor.

6. He needs aspirin. _____ head hurts.

6 **Look at the picture. Complete the sentences. Use __his__ or __her__ and the correct relationship.**

1. Cora is not Najib's daughter.

   She is _his wife_.

2. Martin is not Elly's husband.

   He is _____ _____.

3. Najib is not Martin's brother.

   He is _____ _____.

4. Cora is not Martin's manager.

   She is _____ _____.

5. Elly is not Najib's son.

   She is _____ _____.

Najib   Cora

Martin   Elly

7 **➤CHALLENGE Complete the paragraph. Use __their__, __they're__, or __there__.**

___There___ are two people from Ukraine in my class. _____ names are Ernest
                1.   2.

and Nadia. _____ engineers. _____ studying English this year because
                    3.   4.

_____ son, Alexei, speaks English in school.
        5.

8 ▶ *CHALLENGE* **Combine the sentences. Make one sentence. Use a possessive.**

1. Jimmy has a shirt. It's blue. <u>Jimmy's shirt is blue.</u>

2. Consuelo has a brother. He is a doctor. _____

3. Quan has a computer. It's out of order. _____

4. Marco has an office. It's new. _____

5. Mike has two sisters. They are late. _____

9 **Complete the chart about <u>yourself</u>. Check ☑ <u>never</u>, <u>sometimes</u>, or <u>always</u>.**

	never	sometimes	always
eat American food			
drive to work			
take aspirin			
have a cold			
go to the doctor			

Now write sentences about <u>yourself</u>. Use the information in the chart.

Examples: <u>I sometimes eat American food.</u>

<u>I never go to the doctor.</u>

1. _____

2. _____

3. _____

4. _____

5. _____

10 ▶ *CHALLENGE* **Write sentences. Use the present continuous or the simple present tense.**

1. Alex / always / eat / green apples <u>Alex always eats green apples.</u>

2. Sam / look for /the manager / right now _____

3. Jamal / stay home / today _____

4. Lety's daughter / never / eat / tomatoes _____

5. Ivan / need / a personal day tomorrow _____

➤ Authentic practice

11 **Read. Choose <u>your</u> response. Circle the letter.**

1. "Good morning. Can I talk to Nicky?"

   a. I'm sorry. I'm busy.   **b.** I'm sorry. She's busy.

2. "Dr. Hirano's office."

   a. Hello. This is Alonso.   **b.** Hello. I am Alonso.

3. "I'm really busy. Can you call back later?"

   a. Sure. Feel better!   **b.** Sure. How about at noon?

4. "We need a fire truck at 1216 Edwards Street."

   a. How can I help you?   **b.** It's on its way.

5. "How may I help you?"

   a. I need to make an appointment.   **b.** A fire truck, please.

12 **Complete the conversation. Write the letter on the line.**

1. This is the 911 dispatcher.   _*d*_   **a.** No. No fire.

2. All right, sir. What's the address?   _____   **b.** Thank you.

3. Do they need an ambulance?   _____   **c.** 830 Pine Street. Between

4. And do you see a fire?   _____   32nd Street and 33rd Street.

5. OK. They're on their way.   _____   **d.** There's an accident across

                                                         from my office!

                                                      e. Yes. One driver hurt his arm.

13 Read the conversation. Then check ☑ <u>yes</u> or <u>no</u>.

Mother: Well, honey, I don't think you can go to school today.

Esad: What?

Mother: You need to stay home today.

Esad: Why?

Mother: Because you have a cold, and now you have a fever.

Esad: OK. But you have to write a note to my teacher.

Mother: Yes, I know. What is your teacher's name?

Esad: Mrs. Jacobson.

Mother: OK. I can write the note right now, and your sister can give it to the school office.

Esad: Can I go to school tomorrow?

Mother: I don't know. We'll see later.

	yes	no
1. Esad can go to school today.	❏	❏
2. Esad can't go to school because he has a backache.	❏	❏
3. Esad has to write a note.	❏	❏
4. Mrs. Jacobson is Esad's teacher.	❏	❏
5. Esad's sister can go to school today.	❏	❏

14 Look at the conversation in Exercise 13 again. Complete the note to Esad's teacher.

February 8, 2002

Dear _____,

My son, Esad Balovic, can't _____

_____. He has _____.

He also has_____.

Thank you,

Mrs. Balovic

2314 Baltic Street, #14A

Chicago, IL 60618

(312) 555-7249

15 Complete the patient information form for Esad. Use the information in Exercises 13 and 14. Esad's date of birth is November 11, 1993.

S. Bellugi, MD

Patient Information Sheet

Patient's name: _____
                   last   first

Date of birth: _____ / _____ / _____
           month   day   year

Address: _____
         number   street   apt. #

_____
        city   state   zip code

Phone number: (_____)_____   Today's date: _____ / _____ / _____
                                        month   day   year

What is wrong?_____

16 Read the accident report.

Green Hills Landscaping

Employee Accident Report Form

Employee's name: _Greta Ulwig_   Employee ID number: _380-95-6124_

Date of birth: _6 / 2 / 79_   Doctor's name: _Dr. S. Kangi_

Date of accident: _2 / 6 / 02_   Time of accident: _3:40 p.m._

Describe the injury: _I hurt my ankle._

Location of accident (check one)   ☑ at work   ☐ other

Complete the sentences. Write the letter on the line.

1. The employee's last name is _____.

2. The employee's first name is _____.

3. Her doctor's last name is _____.

4. The employee's date of birth is _____.

5. The date of the accident is _____.

6. The employee hurt her ankle _____.

a. Greta

b. at work

c. Ulwig

d. Kangi

e. June 2, 1979

f. February 6, 2002

17 Read about Sylvia Alaniz. Then complete Sylvia's accident report.

Sylvia Alaniz had an accident on February 3, 2002. She was fixing a lawn mower at work. At 10:30 a.m., she hurt her hand. Her date of birth is April 27, 1952. Sylvia's employee ID number is 494-40-3301. Her doctor is Dr. Carol Buxbaum.

Green Hills Landscaping

Employee Accident Report Form

Employee's name: _____   Employee ID number: _____

Date of birth: _____   Doctor's name: _____

Date of accident: _____   Time of accident: _____

Describe the injury: _____

Location of accident (check one)   ☐ at work   ☐ other

UNIT 9

Money

➤ Vocabulary

1 Circle the word that doesn't match.

1. a money order   (cheap)   a credit card   cash

2. a check   expensive   cheap   new

3. a bill   a check   a money order   cash

4. a check   a money order   an ATM   a credit card

5. charge   go shopping   pay cash   pay by mail

2 Complete the chart. Write the amount.

1.		$.75
2.		$
3.		$
4.		$
5.		$

3 Complete the sentences. Use your <u>own</u> places.

Example: I cash my checks at *First State Bank.*

1. I cash my checks at _____.

2. _____ is a cheap store.

3. _____ is an expensive store.

➤ Practical conversations

4 **Put the words in order. Write sentences.**

1. you / change / a / Do / dollar / have / for / ?

   Do you have change for a dollar?

2. these / much / pants / How / are / ?

   _____

3. it / have / about / I'll / to / think / .

   _____

4. expensive / computer / too / That / is / .

   _____

5. cash / Will / charge / or / be / that / ?

   _____

5 **Complete the conversation. Use the pictures or your <u>own</u> words.**

A: Excuse me. How much is this _____?

B: That _____? It's_____.

A: Is it on sale?

B: _____.

A: OK. I'll take it. And how much are the _____?

B: _____.

A: Hm. That's _____. I'll have to think about it.

B: OK. And will that be cash or charge?

A: _____.

➤ Practical grammar

6 **Complete the sentences. Use a form of <u>be going to</u> and the verb. Write the words on the line.**

1. We <u>'re going to go</u> _____ to California next month.

    go

2. The class _____ at 5:50.

    start

3. _____ you _____ that microwave? It's too small.

    return

4. When _____ Danny _____ the doctor?

    call

5. I _____ this bill by mail.

    pay

7 **Complete the sentences. Write the letter on the line.**

1. Keiko _____ the restrooms tomorrow.

   a. cleaning   **b.** is going to clean

2. Alicia and Tom always _____ in the computer room.

   a. study   **b.** are going to study

3. Mi-son never _____ to work early.

   a. is coming   **b.** comes

4. _____ that TV or are you going to write a check?

   a. Do you charge   **b.** Are you going to charge

5. When is that new store _____?

   a. opens   **b.** going to open

8 **Complete the questions. Write <u>Whose</u> or <u>Who's</u>.**

1. _____ receipt book is this? It doesn't have a name.

2. _____ going to be ready in 15 minutes?

3. _____ phone number do you need—Anna's or Helena's?

4. _____ computer are you going to fix first?

5. _____ going to go to the bank? We need some change.

6. _____ driving the school bus this year—Ms. Jaross or a new driver?

9 ▶ *CHALLENGE* **Look at the answers. Write questions. Use words from the box and your own words.**

~~How many~~	Whose	How much	Why	Where

1. **A:** *How many bills do you have to pay today?*

   B: I have to pay 3 bills today.

2. **A:** _____

   B: The answering machine is $34.99.

3. **A:** _____

   B: They're going to Car City USA.

4. **A:** _____

   B: She's driving her mother's car.

5. **A:** _____

   B: Haile can't cash his paycheck because the bank isn't open.

10 **Complete the sentences. Use your own words.**

1. Tomorrow I'm going to _____.

2. I'm going to _____ on Sunday.

3. Next month I'm going to _____.

➤ Authentic practice

11 **Complete the conversations. Circle the letter.**

1. **A:** This cold medicine is not cheap!

   B: How much is it?

   A: **a.** Great!   **b.** It's $13.99.   **c.** I'll take it.

2. **A:** I'll take it.

   B: Great. Cash or charge?

   A: **a.** No.   **b.** Here you go.   **c.** Cash.

3. **A:** What are you going to do on Saturday?

   B: I'm going to go shopping. How about you?

   A: **a.** Me too. I want   **b.** Not me. I have   **c.** Not me. I have to
   to pay my bills.   a credit card.   pay my old bills first.

4. **A:** How much is that jacket?

   B: The red one? It's $129, on sale.

   A: **a.** Let me check.   **b.** Thanks. I'll have   **c.** OK. Will that be
                              to think about it.   cash or charge?

5. **A:** I need a cheap car.

   B: How much do you want to pay?

   A: **a.** $3,000.   **b.** Is a check OK?   **c.** Cash.

12 ➤CHALLENGE **Look at the electric bill. Look at the <u>underlined</u> words.**

		Amount due
		$46.20

Evergreen Power and Electric Company

Phuong Lam
329 E. Anchor St.
Middleton, OR 90610

		Date due
		3/31/03

Billing period	Number of days	Date of this bill
2/8/03 - 3/8/03	28	3/10/03

After 3/31/03, this bill is <u>overdue</u>. There is a <u>late charge</u> of $3.50 after 3/31/03.

What do the <u>underlined</u> words mean? Write the <u>underlined</u> words on the line.

1. The date the bill starts to the date the bill ends = *billing period*

2. The money Phuong has to pay = _____

3. The money Phuong has to pay if her check is late = _____

4. The date Phuong has to pay the bill = _____

5. Late = _____

13 **Look at the sign for the Motor Vehicle Administration. Then check ☑ <u>true</u> or <u>false</u>.**

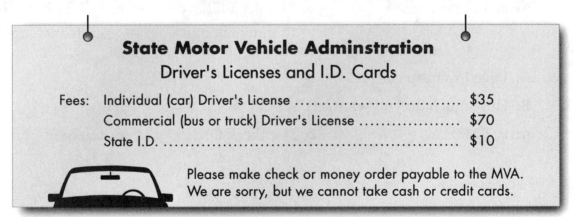

State Motor Vehicle Adminstration
Driver's Licenses and I.D. Cards

Fees: Individual (car) Driver's License $35
Commercial (bus or truck) Driver's License $70
State I.D. $10

Please make check or money order payable to the MVA.
We are sorry, but we cannot take cash or credit cards.

	true	false
1. A driver's license for a car is $70.	❑	❑
2. An I.D. card is $10.	❑	❑
3. You can pay for a driver's license with a money order.	❑	❑
4. You can pay for a driver's license with cash.	❑	❑
5. The MVA is the Motor Vehicle Administration.	❑	❑

14 Look at the sign in Exercise 13 again. Andrea Solis is getting a state I.D. card at the MVA. She is going to pay for the I.D. card by check. Write the check for Andrea. Use today's date.

Andrea Solis   152
1624 N. 14ᵗʰ St., Apt. 6
San Jose, CA 95132   DATE _____

PAY TO THE
ORDER OF _____ | $ _____

_____ DOLLARS

First City Bank
328 Lexington Avenue
San Jose, CA 95132
                                                      Andrea Solis

MEMO _____

⑆420220089⑆ 80600668' 152

15 Look at the check and credit card policy. Answer the customers' questions. Use the information in the policy and your <u>own</u> words.

Super Cash-Mart
Check and Credit Card Policy

• We accept credit cards and debit cards.
• We accept money orders.
• We accept checks, but you must have our store check-cashing card to write a check.
• Go to the Customer Service desk for a check-cashing card.
• Sorry, we do not cash paychecks.

1. **Customer:** Can I pay with a money order?

   (YOU) *Yes, you can* _____ .

2. **Customer:** I'm going to write a check. Do you need to see my I.D.?

   (YOU) No, but you need _____ .

3. **Customer:** I want to charge this. Do you take credit cards?

   (YOU) _____ .

4. **Customer:** I don't have a check-cashing card. Where can I get one?

   (YOU) _____ .

5. **Customer:** Can you cash my paycheck?

   (YOU) _____ .

16 **Complete the directions for an ATM. Use words from the box.**

cash	take	P.I.N.	press	ATM card	receipt

1. Please insert your _____.

2. What language do you want to use? Please
   _____ <u>English</u> or <u>Spanish</u>.

3. Please enter your _____
   (Personal Identification Number).

4. Please enter the amount of
   _____ you want.

5. Please _____ your cash.

6. Please take your _____.

UNIT 10

Your career

➤ Vocabulary

1 **Complete the sentences. Use words from the box.**

receptionist	telephone technician	helps nurses	dishwasher
plumber	take care of children	dental assistant	hairdresser

1. Lola is a nurse's aide. She _____.

2. Brian is a _____. He greets visitors in an office.

3. Angie and Thi are child care workers. They _____.

4. Milek washes dishes in a restaurant. He is a _____.

5. Andres fixes sinks and toilets. He is a _____.

6. Marina is a _____. She helps a dentist in her office.

7. Aldo cuts my hair. He is a _____.

8. Choi fixes and installs telephones. He is a _____.

2 **Complete the chart. Write occupations.**

Workplace	Occupations
1. a hospital	*a nurse,*
2. a restaurant	
3. a store	
4. an office	

➤ Practical conversations

3 **Put the conversation in order. Write the number on the line.**

___1___ Hello. I'm looking for a job.

_____ Well, not really. But I was a cashier in my family's store in Somalia.

___2___ Great. What skills do you have?

_____ A cashier! That's interesting. Do you want to fill out an application today?

_____ I'm a good worker, and I like to help people.

_____ Yes, thanks.

_____ Good. Do you have any experience in this country?

4 **Complete the conversation. Use your own words.**

A: What skills do you have?

B: I can _____ and _____.

A: What did you do in _____?

B: I was _____.

A: _____! That's interesting. How long did you do that?

B: _____.

A: And are you working right now?

B: _____.

A: OK. What was your last job?

B: I was _____.

➤ Practical grammar

5 **Complete the sentences. Choose a word. Write the word on the line.**

1. I _____ a nurse's aide in my country. Now I'm a dental assistant.
   was / were / am

2. Andy _____ at work today. He was at home.
   was / were / wasn't

3. Boris and Irene _____ unemployed last year. They were cashiers.
   was / were / weren't

4. You _____ early three days last week. That's great!
   was / were / wasn't

5. The car _____ expensive. It was really cheap.
   was / were / wasn't

6 **Look at the answers. Write questions. Use the past tense of be.**

1. A: Where _was the accident?_____

   B: The accident was on First Street.

2. A: Why _____

   B: They were late because their bus was late.

3. A: When _____

   B: Luba's interview was on Tuesday.

4. A: Who _____

   B: The manager was at the meeting.

5. A: How long _____

   B: They were in Peru for two years.

7 Complete the sentences. Use the simple past tense. Write the words on the line.

1. Antonio _____ a truck in Portugal, but now he's a taxi driver.

drive

2. At her last job, Molly _____ cash registers and copiers.

fix

3. We _____ our house. We _____ a house painter.

not paintpay

4. I _____ yesterday. I _____ time.

not studynot have

5. I _____ to cash a check yesterday, so I _____ to

wantgo

the bank.

8 Look at the answers. Complete the questions. Use the simple past tense. Write the words on the line.

1. A: Where _did you eat_____?

you / eat

   B: At a small Chinese restaurant.

2. A: Who _____?

fix / coffee machine

   B: Janna.

3. A: _____ your old job?

you / like

   B: No, I didn't. It wasn't interesting.

4. A: When _____ this job?

you / start

   B: In February.

5. A: _____ these pictures?

the children / paint

   B: Yes, they did.

9 Answer the questions. Use your <u>own</u> words.

1. Were you a student last year? _____

2. What did you do in your country? _____

3. Did you study English in your country? _____

4. What did you do yesterday? _____

➤ Authentic practice

10 Read. Choose <u>your</u> response. Circle the letter.

1. "So, I see that you were a hairdresser in China."

   a. Yes, I was.   **b.** Yes, I am.

2. "What experience do you have?"

   a. Well, not really.   **b.** Well, I was a driver for three years in Cuba.

3. "Can you use a cash register?"

   a. For two years.   **b.** Not really, but I learn fast.

4. "Tell me—what did you do last year?"

   a. I was unemployed.   **b.** I can install telephones.

5. "How long did you work in Venezuela?"

   a. For eight years.   **b.** In eight years.

11 Complete the conversation. Write the letter on the line.

1. We're looking for a cook's helper.   _*f*_

2. We need a person to cut vegetables and help the cooks. Can you do that? _____

3. Do you have any restaurant experience? _____

4. What other skills do you have? _____

5. And when are you available to start? _____

6. Did you fill out an application? _____

   a. Not really, but I cook for my family.

   b. Tomorrow.

   c. Not yet, but I can do it now.

   d. I'm a good worker, and I learn fast.

   e. Yes, I can.

   f. Can you tell me about the job?

12 Read the sign. Check ☑ <u>true</u> or <u>false</u>.

1. The restaurant needs one new worker.

   true ☐   **false** ☐

2. Monique Peltier was a cashier in Haiti.
   She can apply for the cashier job.

   true ☐   **false** ☐

3. Monique can apply for the dishwasher job.

   true ☐   **false** ☐

4. The dishwasher job is part-time.

   true ☐   **false** ☐

5. Alberto Goncalvez doesn't have any experience.
   He can apply at the restaurant.

   true ☐   **false** ☐

6. Alberto and Monique can apply at the restaurant at 10:00 a.m.

   true ☐   **false** ☐

Help Wanted

2 positions

CASHIER (part-time: 10:00 a.m. – 2:00 p.m.)

Experience required

DISHWASHER (full-time: 3:00 p.m. – 11:30 p.m.)

No experience necessary

Apply inside between 3:00 p.m. and 7:00 p.m.

13 ► *CHALLENGE* **Look at the ads. Read about the people. Complete the sentences.**

> Martin Chen was a nurse in Taiwan. He needs a full-time job. He has two children. His wife's job starts at 4:00 p.m. Martin has to be home at 3:00 p.m. to take care of his children.

1. Martin can't apply for this job because he has to be

   home <u>*at 3:00 p.m.*</u>   .

   Company: ___Office of___
   ___Dr. Jose Mendoza___
   Position: <u>Nurse</u>
   <u>Experience is required</u>
   ☐ Part-time   ☑ Full-time
   Hours: <u>10:00 a.m. to 5:00 p.m.</u>
   Call 555-2380 for an
   interview.

2. Martin can apply for this job because it ends

   _____.

   Company: <u>General Hospital</u>

   Position: <u>Nurse's aide</u>

   ☐ Part-time   ☑ Full-time
   Hours: <u>6:00 a.m. to 2:00 p.m.</u>
   Experience required.
   Apply at 30 River Road.

3. Can <u>you</u> apply for this job? Complete the sentence.

   Use your own words.

   Example: <u>*No, I can't,*</u> because <u>*I don't*</u>

   <u>*have any experience.*</u>

   _____, because _____.

Suni Sanji was a homemaker for eight years. Now she is looking for a job. She is a good worker, but she doesn't have any experience. She wants a part-time job.

4. Suni _____ apply for this job because the hotel doesn't require _____.

Good Neighbor Direct • 4338 DiPaolo Center, Glenview IL 60025 • (800) 772-2229

Good Neighbor FREE AD

Position: Housekeeper | Phone
Part-time
Hours: 7:00 a.m. to 12:00 p.m. | Phone
No experience required.
Apply at the 100 Garden
Street entrance. | Phone

Name Northview Hotel Date_____ | Phone

5. Suni _____ apply for this job because she doesn't _____.

6. Can <u>you</u> apply for this job? Complete the sentence. Use your own words.

_____, because _____

_____.

Good Neighbor Direct • 4338 DiPaolo Center, Glenview IL 60025 • (800) 772-2229

Good Neighbor FREE AD

Position: Teacher's aide | Phone
6 months experience in a
school or child care center | Phone
required.
Part-time
8:00 a.m. – 1:00 p.m. | Phone
Call 555-1608 for interview.
Ask for Mrs. Chao. | Phone

Name Early-Learning Pre-School

14 ►*CHALLENGE* **Read about Ari Panos. Then complete the job application for Ari.**

Ari Panos is from Greece. He was a cashier at the Main Post Office on the island of Naxos. He helped customers and used a cash register. He worked there from 1994 to 2000.

Now Ari is working in a Greek restaurant in Austin, Texas. The restaurant's name is Blue Cafe. Ari is a dishwasher. He washes dishes and cleans the kitchen. He started this job in June, 2001. Ari wants a new job at Mail and More.

Mail and More
JOB APPLICATION

Applicant: _____

Please list your last job first.

Employer	Address or location	Duties or skills	Dates
	Austin, Texas		
Main Post Office			

15 > *CHALLENGE* **Answer the interviewer's questions. Use your name and a job you are interested in. Use your own words.**

Interviewer: Hello, _____. I understand you are interested
(your first name)

in the _____ opening.
(a job you want)

YOU Yes, I am.

Interviewer: That's good. Do you have any experience?

YOU _____.

Interviewer: OK. What skills do you have?

YOU _____.

Interviewer: Good. Now, what was your last job?

YOU _____.

Interviewer: And where was that?

YOU _____.

Interviewer: How long did you do that?

YOU _____.

Interviewer: Are you working now?

YOU _____.

Interviewer: And when could you start work here?

YOU _____.

Interviewer: Very good. Thank you for coming. It was nice to meet you.

YOU _____.

Skills for test taking

Write your information in the boxes. Fill in the ovals.

LAST NAME	FIRST NAME	MI

A B C D E F G H I J K L M N O P Q R S T U V W X Y Z (ovals for each letter across all name columns)

DATE OF BIRTH		
Month	Day	Year 19__
Jan	0 0	0 0
Feb	1 1	1 1
Mar	2 2	2 2
Apr	3 3	3 3
May	4	4 4
Jun	5	5 5
Jul	6	6 6
Aug	7	7 7
Sep	8	8 8
Oct	9	9 9
Nov		
Dec		

TELEPHONE NUMBER
0 0 0 0 0 0 0 0 0 0
1 1 1 1 1 1 1 1 1 1
2 2 2 2 2 2 2 2 2 2
3 3 3 3 3 3 3 3 3 3
4 4 4 4 4 4 4 4 4 4
5 5 5 5 5 5 5 5 5 5
6 6 6 6 6 6 6 6 6 6
7 7 7 7 7 7 7 7 7 7
8 8 8 8 8 8 8 8 8 8
9 9 9 9 9 9 9 9 9 9

TODAY'S DATE		
Month	Day	Year 20__
Jan	0 0	0 0
Feb	1 1	1 1
Mar	2 2	2 2
Apr	3 3	3
May	4	4
Jun	5	5
Jul	6	6
Aug	7	7
Sep	8	8
Oct	9	9
Nov		
Dec		

Unit 1

Choose an answer.

City Center Adult School

DATE: _2/24/01_

NAME: _Batista_   _Pedro_
      Last Name   First Name

ADDRESS: _368 King Street_   _Fort Worth_   _TX_   _76101_
         Number and Street   City   State   ZIP Code

TELEPHONE: (_682_) _555-2301_   NATIONALITY: _Brazilian_

OCCUPATION: _Mechanic_   COURSE: _English 1A_

1. A. Pedro Batista is a teacher.
   B. Pedro Batista is a mechanic.
   C. Pedro Batista is not a mechanic.

2. A. Pedro Batista is from Brazil.
   B. Pedro Batista is from King Street.
   C. Pedro Batista is from England.

NEW Student News

Garden Street Adult School

Please welcome Hai Tan to our English class. Hai is from Vietnam. She is a cook.

3. A. Hai Tan is a cook.
   B. Hai Tan is a teacher.
   C. Hai Tan is English.

1. Ⓐ Ⓑ Ⓒ

2. Ⓐ Ⓑ Ⓒ

3. Ⓐ Ⓑ Ⓒ

List of Employees

Manager	Jin Park	**Housekeepers**	Ming Chao
Cashiers	Tina Reyes		Ana Gomez
	Adam Moore		Alan Smith
		Engineer	Tony Vargas

4. Where is the list from?

    A.   The list is from Jin Park.

    B.   The list is from the Villa Hotel.

    C.   The list is from the employees.

5. Is Adam Moore unemployed right now?

    A.   Yes, he is.

    B.   No, he's not. He's a manager.

    C.   No, he's not. He's a cashier.

4. Ⓐ Ⓑ Ⓒ

5. Ⓐ Ⓑ Ⓒ

Unit 2

Choose an answer.

supermarket	parking lot	restaurant	

First Street

- -

bank	school	post office	hospital

1. Where is the school?

   A.   It's next to the parking lot.
   B.   It's between the supermarket and the bank.
   C.   It's across from the parking lot.

2. What's next to the restaurant?

   A.   The post office.
   B.   The parking lot.
   C.   The hospital.

1. Ⓐ Ⓑ Ⓒ

2. Ⓐ Ⓑ Ⓒ

The **Friends Restaurant** is looking for new employees.

INTERVIEWS:
Saturday, March 18
Sunday, March 19
1 p.m. to 5 p.m.

JOBS OPEN:

Cashiers • Cooks • Managers

2535 Bank Street, Lincoln, FL 33105

3. A. The restaurant is looking for housekeepers.
    B. The restaurant is looking for engineers.
    C. The restaurant is looking for cooks.

4. A. The restaurant is on Bank Street.
    B. The restaurant is on Lincoln Street.
    C. The restaurant is next to the bank.

3. Ⓐ Ⓑ Ⓒ

4. Ⓐ Ⓑ Ⓒ

Unit 3

Choose an answer.

Directions:
Close the lid.
Press the <u>start</u> button.

1. How do you start the copier?

   A.   Press the <u>on</u> button.
   B.   Press the <u>off</u> button.
   C.   Press the <u>start</u> button.

2. Where are the directions?

   A.   On the copier.
   B.   On the lid.
   C.   On the right.

1. Ⓐ Ⓑ Ⓒ

2. Ⓐ Ⓑ Ⓒ

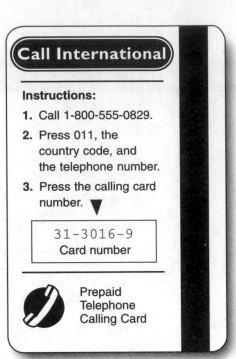

Call International

Instructions:

1. Call 1-800-555-0829.

2. Press 011, the country code, and the telephone number.

3. Press the calling card number. ▼

> 31-3016-9
> Card number

Prepaid Telephone Calling Card

3. A. This is a telephone.
   B. This is a phone card.
   C. This is a card number.

4. A. The card number is 011.
   B. The card number is 1-800-555-0829.
   C. The card number is 31-3016-9.

3. Ⓐ Ⓑ Ⓒ

4. Ⓐ Ⓑ Ⓒ

Unit 4

Choose an answer.

A-1 Office Supplies

Exchange Department

Name: _Martiza Pena_

Item: _coffee maker_

Reason for return: _wrong size – too small_

Salesperson: _Genet Wolde_

1. Who is Martiza Pena?

   A. She is the customer.
   B. She is the cashier.
   C. She is the salesperson.

2. Who is Genet Wolde?

   A. She is the customer.
   B. She is the cashier.
   C. She is the salesperson.

3. What's the problem?

   A. The coffee maker is the wrong color.
   B. The coffee maker is too small.
   C. The coffee maker is too large.

1. Ⓐ Ⓑ Ⓒ

2. Ⓐ Ⓑ Ⓒ

3. Ⓐ Ⓑ Ⓒ

West Avenue Clothes

REFUND AND EXCHANGE POLICY

Refunds and exchanges for
customers with receipts.

4. Floretta Smith wants to return a
   jacket. What does she need?

   A. She needs a customer.
   B. She needs an exchange.
   C. She needs her receipt.

5. Does the store give refunds?

   A. No.
   B. Yes.
   C. I don't know.

4. Ⓐ Ⓑ Ⓒ

5. Ⓐ Ⓑ Ⓒ

Unit 5

Choose an answer.

Metro Theaters

Name: _Fanta Rivera_

Schedule: 6:00 p.m. – 1:00 a.m.

TIME CARD

Day		In
MONDAY	AUGUST 19	5:45 p.m.
TUESDAY	AUGUST 20	6:00 p.m.
WEDNESDAY	AUGUST 21	5:55 p.m.
THURSDAY	AUGUST 22	6:05 p.m.
FRIDAY	AUGUST 23	5:55 p.m.

1. A.   It's 10:10.
   B.   It's 2:50.
   C.   It's 2:10.

2. A. On Thursday, Fanta Rivera is on time.
   B. On Thursday, Fanta Rivera is early.
   C. On Thursday, Fanta Rivera is late.

1. Ⓐ Ⓑ Ⓒ

2. Ⓐ Ⓑ Ⓒ

Post Office Hours

**Monday to Friday
8 a.m. – 5 p.m.**

**Saturday
9 a.m. – 1 p.m.**

3. What time does the post office open
   on Tuesday?

   A. At 8 a.m.
   B. At 9 a.m.
   C. At 5 p.m.

4. What time does the post office close
   on Saturday?

   A. At 5 p.m.
   B. At 9 a.m.
   C. At 1 p.m.

5. When is the post office open?

   A. Monday to Friday.
   B. Monday to Saturday.
   C. Saturday to Sunday.

3. Ⓐ Ⓑ Ⓒ

4. Ⓐ Ⓑ Ⓒ

5. Ⓐ Ⓑ Ⓒ

Unit 6

Choose an answer.

_____ *Shopping List* _____

Mitch –
We need lettuce, eggs, bread,
apple juice, chicken soup, and rice.
Thanks,
Donna

1. What's on the shopping list?

    A. Bread, apple juice, and chicken.
    B. Bread, apples, and rice.
    C. Bread, apple juice, and rice.
    D. Bread, apples, chicken soup, and rice.

2. How many foods and drinks do Mitch and Donna need?

    A. 4
    B. 6
    C. 7
    D. 8

3. Is there any fish on Mitch's shopping list?

    A. Yes, there is.
    B. Yes, there are.
    C. No, there aren't.
    D. No, there isn't.

1. Ⓐ Ⓑ Ⓒ Ⓓ

2. Ⓐ Ⓑ Ⓒ Ⓓ

3. Ⓐ Ⓑ Ⓒ Ⓓ

Black Bean Soup

Ingredients

1 medium onion

2 small tomatoes

2 tablespoons of oil

2 10-ounce cans of
Cuban black beans

1 cup of water

Directions

1. Chop the onion.
2. Put the onion and the oil in a pot. Cook for 5 minutes.
3. Chop the tomatoes. Put the tomatoes in the pot.
4. Put the beans and the water in the pot. Cook for 20 minutes.

4. A. Cook the water first.
   B. Cook the beans first.
   C. Cook the tomatoes first.
   D. Cook the onion first.

5. A. You need two tomatoes for this recipe.
   B. You need one tomato for this recipe.
   C. You need tomato juice for this recipe.
   D. You need tomato soup for this recipe.

4. Ⓐ Ⓑ Ⓒ Ⓓ

5. Ⓐ Ⓑ Ⓒ Ⓓ

Unit 7

Choose an answer.

Super Shoes

Personal Day Policy

- Employees may take 3 personal days in one year.
- You must fill out a personal day form 1 day <u>before</u> your personal day.
- Write the date of your personal day on the form.
- Write the date you can return to work.
- Take the form to your manager.

1. Who has to fill out the personal day form?

    A. The store manager.
    B. The employee.
    C. The manager.
    D. The salesperson.

2. Kayo Hirano wants to take a personal day on November 11. When does she have to fill out a personal day form?

    A. On November 10.
    B. On November 11.
    C. On November 8.
    D. On November 3.

3. What does Kayo Hirano have to write on her personal day form?

    A. Her address.
    B. The date.
    C. The date of her personal day.
    D. Her manager's name.

1. Ⓐ Ⓑ Ⓒ Ⓓ

2. Ⓐ Ⓑ Ⓒ Ⓓ

3. Ⓐ Ⓑ Ⓒ Ⓓ

Shop Time Supermarket 🛒   Personal Day Form

Employee: _____ *Mario Bello* _____

Today's date: _____ **October 5** _____   Date(s) of personal day(s): _____ *October 6* _____

Reason: _____ *I have to take my mother to the doctor.* _____

---

4. A. Mario Bello's personal day is October 5.
   B. Mario Bello's personal day is October 6.
   C. Mario Bello's personal day is October 7.
   D. Mario Bello's personal day is today.

5. A. Mario needs a personal day because he has to work.
   B. Mario needs a personal day because he has to go to the hospital.
   C. Mario needs a personal day because he has to go to the supermarket.
   D. Mario needs a personal day because he has to take his mother to the doctor.

4. Ⓐ Ⓑ Ⓒ Ⓓ

5. Ⓐ Ⓑ Ⓒ Ⓓ

Unit 8

Choose an answer.

Dr. Akrim Malouf

90 S. Roberts Road, Palm Ridge, Florida 33110

Patient ___*Mari Olsen*___ has an appointment on

☑ Mon ☐ Tues ☐ Wed ☐ Thurs ☐ Fri

___*1/6/03*___ at ___*1:00 p.m.*___

Please call (309) 555-1780 if you cannot keep this appointment.

---

1. Who needs to go to the doctor?

    A. Akrim Malouf.
    B. Mari Olsen.
    C. Dr. Malouf.
    D. Ms. Roberts.

2. When is the appointment?

    A. On Monday, January 6.
    B. On Monday, January 3.
    C. On Monday, June 1.
    D. On Monday, June 3.

1. Ⓐ Ⓑ Ⓒ Ⓓ

2. Ⓐ Ⓑ Ⓒ Ⓓ

MacBride Tools, Inc.

Factory Health Clinic

Patient's name: **Simone** **Blanc**   Date of visit: **12** **6** **01**
                 first   last or family   month   day   year

Address: **1904 Chestnut St.,**   **Anchorage**   **AK**   **99505**
             number and street   city   state   zip code

Date of birth: **7** **4** **52**   Telephone: **(907)** **555-1617**
          month   day   year   area code   number

Injury is to:		Place of accident:	Fever?	Headache?
☐ back	☐ ankle	☑ at home	☐ yes	☐ yes
☐ neck	☐ foot	☐ at work	☑ no	☑ no
☑ hand	☐ head	☐ car accident		
☐ wrist	☐ other			
☐ leg				

3. A. Simone Blanc had an accident in her car.
   B. Simone Blanc hurt her hand at work.
   C. Simone Blanc hurt her hand at home.
   D. Simone Blanc hurt her head at home.

4. A. Simone has a fever and a headache.
   B. Simone has a fever. She doesn't have a headache.
   C. Simone doesn't have a fever. She has a headache.
   D. Simone doesn't have a fever. She doesn't have a headache.

3. Ⓐ Ⓑ Ⓒ Ⓓ

4. Ⓐ Ⓑ Ⓒ Ⓓ

Unit 9

Choose an answer.

```
Chien Hsu                                              299
250 W. 85TH Street
New York, NY 10025              DATE   6/17/03

PAY TO THE    Troy's Market                    | $   83.03
ORDER OF
              Eighty - three and  03                  DOLLARS
                                 ─────
                                  100
NY Bank
2560 BROADWAY AT 96TH STREET
NEW YORK, NY  10025

MEMO _____ food _____              Chien Hsu

3: 34035009:1   2001558' 299
```

1. What is Chien Hsu buying?

   A. A market.
   B. A check.
   C. Food.
   D. Cash.

2. How much is Chien Hsu paying?

   A. $2.99
   B. $83.03
   C. $6.17
   D. $261.00

1. Ⓐ Ⓑ Ⓒ Ⓓ

2. Ⓐ Ⓑ Ⓒ Ⓓ

Western Wireless Phone Services

P.O. Box 1381, Vista, NV 89126

CUSTOMER SERVICE NUMBER
1-800-555-1953

ACCOUNT NUMBER
22579-1430

‖‖ⅈ‖‖‖ⅈ‖ⅈ‖ⅈ‖

Raul Hernandez
26B N. Canton
Vista, NV   89126

BILLING PERIOD	PAY BY	AMOUNT DUE	AMOUNT DUE AFTER 6/3/02
4/15/02 to 5/14/02	6/3/02	$36.25	$38.17

3. Raul Hernandez pays the bill on May 31. He pays _____.

   A. $36.25
   B. $38.17
   C. $38.25
   D. $36.17

4. The phone bill is for _____.

   A. one week
   B. one month
   C. two months
   D. one year

5. 22579-1430 is _____.

   A. Raul Hernandez's phone bill
   B. the customer service phone number
   C. Raul Hernandez's account number
   D. Raul Hernandez's phone number

3. Ⓐ Ⓑ Ⓒ Ⓓ

4. Ⓐ Ⓑ Ⓒ Ⓓ

5. Ⓐ Ⓑ Ⓒ Ⓓ

Unit 10

Choose an answer.

SALLY'S SUSHI

Help Wanted

Cook (one position).
Full-time, evenings.
Experience required.

Dishwasher (one position).
Part-time, evenings.
No experience required.

Cashier (two positions).
Part-time, afternoons.
No experience required.

Please ask inside the restaurant.

1. How many new employees does the restaurant need?

   A. One.
   B. Two.
   C. Three.
   D. Four.

2. Jim Farkas has no experience. What jobs can he apply for?

   A. The cook and the dishwasher.
   B. The cashier and the dishwasher.
   C. The cook.
   D. He can't apply for these jobs.

1. Ⓐ Ⓑ Ⓒ Ⓓ

2. Ⓐ Ⓑ Ⓒ Ⓓ

Applicant: _Solange Pierre_		Position: _nurse's aide_	
Employer or place	**Job**	**Experience or skills**	**Dates**
Early Start Day Care, Bangor, Maine	child care worker	take care of children	2001 to now
Dr. Martin's office, Port-au-Prince, Haiti	doctor's assistant	helped doctor and nurses	1995 to 2000

3. A. Solange Pierre took care of children at her job in Haiti.
    B. Solange Pierre helped nurse's aides at Dr. Martin's office.
    C. Solange Pierre takes care of children at her job now.
    D. Solange Pierre helps doctors at her job now.

4. A. Solange was a doctor's assistant in Haiti.
    B. Solange is a doctor's assistant now.
    C. Solange was a doctor's assistant in 2001.
    D. Solange was a doctor's assistant in Maine.

5. A. Solange was a nurse in 1999.
    B. Solange was a doctor's assistant for 5 years.
    C. Solange was a doctor's assistant for 2 years.
    D. Solange worked in Dr. Martin's office last year.

3. Ⓐ Ⓑ Ⓒ Ⓓ

4. Ⓐ Ⓑ Ⓒ Ⓓ

5. Ⓐ Ⓑ Ⓒ Ⓓ